Time Management

Time Management Abilities To Assist You In Achieving More In Life And Managing It More Effectively

(Stress Reduction, Time Optimization, And Increased Productivity Are The Keys To Work-life Balance And Productivity)

Alfonso Sanders

TABLE OF CONTENT

Instruments and Technology 1

Accountability Is Essential for Development 11

Proactive Techniques for Time Management 25

Time management advice. 45

Transcending Stereotypes and Shifting Attitudes .. 69

Examining and Modifying Your Objectives 99

Cut off pointless meetings and concentrate on things that can be done. 122

How can you start telling people no? 148

Instruments and Technology

Technology and Tools' Place in Time Management

We have access to many tools and technologies in the modern world that can aid in time management.

In this chapter, we'll look at a few of the most important tools and technologies that can help boost productivity and efficiency.

Applications for Productivity

You can measure progress, create objectives, and organize your work with numerous productivity applications.

Here are a few well-known instances:

Trello: A platform for managing projects that enables you to make lists and boards to keep track of assignments and deadlines.

Evernote: An application that allows you to take notes in text, picture, and audio formats.

Todoist: An application for creating and prioritizing to-do lists, setting objectives, and setting reminders.

Digital Calendars

Using an electronic calendar to manage appointments, meetings, and events is a good idea.

Among the most widely used electronic calendars are the following:

Google Calendar: An online calendar allowing you to share calendars with others, create events, and set reminders.

Microsoft Outlook: An application for managing emails with a built-in calendar for setting up meetings and appointments.

Apple Calendar: This is the built-in calendar on Apple products, providing comparable functions, including calendar sharing and event creation.

Tools for Time Management

You can track and maximize your time usage with several time management tools.

Here are a few choices:

RescueTime: An application that keeps track of your computer or mobile device usage automatically and generates comprehensive productivity reports.

Focus@Will is a music service that provides a playlist of tracks specifically chosen to boost productivity and is intended to help users focus and concentrate better while working.

Forest is a gamification tool that rewards you for maintaining focus and avoiding distractions by growing a virtual tree every time you complete your activities on time.

Techniques for Managing Emails

An enormous source of distraction and information overload is email.

Discover some methods and resources that can assist you in more effectively controlling the flow of emails:

Zero Input Box: To keep your inbox organized, use the "Inbox Zero" strategy, which involves processing every email right away by archiving, deleting, or answering.

Route them to the relevant folders for easy finding and prioritization, and set up email filters and folders.

Unroll.me: An email subscription management application that makes it simple to stop receiving newsletters and other pointless messages.

After finishing this chapter, you will have a thorough understanding of the tools and technology available to assist you with time management.

Remember that not every tool will work for you, so try out various options to determine which ones best fit your preferences and working style.

There was a young prince named Max who lived in a very, very faraway land. Max was a good-hearted and aspirational prince but frequently had trouble focusing and setting priorities. He often put off vital activities and squandered hours on trivial ones.

Max changed his habits and became more organized and focused one day. He started by clearly defining his short- and long-term objectives. He jotted them down and stuck them somewhere noticeable so he would see them daily.

Max then became aware of the Eisenhower matrix and started using it to arrange his duties in order of importance. He discovered that by grouping his chores, he could concentrate more on the ones that would help him reach his objectives. He made sure to finish tasks as soon as feasible and prioritized those that were urgent and necessary. Important but non-urgent chores were planned ahead of time in his schedule, while important but urgent tasks were assigned to others. All tasks that were neither urgent nor significant were removed.

Max also started to control his distractions better. He delineated boundaries and created a distraction-free designated workstation. He disabled notifications and designated certain times of the day to monitor and reply to messages and emails. In addition, he began utilizing the Pomodoro Technique, which divided work into 25-minute halves and required a 5-minute rest in between. This allowed him to briefly concentrate on a single activity before taking a break to clear his head and refocus.

Additionally, Max started to monitor his energy levels throughout the day and planned his most difficult and significant chores for when he felt most energized. He was careful to take breaks and partake in rejuvenating activities like working out, practicing meditation, or hanging out with friends and family.

Max started to make genuine progress as he kept his attention on his objectives and gave his responsibilities top priority. His realm was thriving, and he could finish more significant responsibilities faster. His students were content, and he had the respect of his friends, family, and peers. He was now a doer rather than just a dreamer.

As word of Max's narrative spread throughout the kingdom, many others started using his techniques for setting priorities and maintaining concentration. Everybody could accomplish their objectives and have more satisfying lives as the kingdom became more efficient and well-organized.

The lesson from Max's experience is that you may be effective in your personal and professional life by establishing clear goals, prioritizing chores, controlling distractions, and being aware of your energy levels. Setting priorities and maintaining focus might be difficult, but they can be mastered with some work and discipline.

As for Max, he rose to prominence as the kingdom's most prosperous ruler in its annals. He provided prosperity and peace to his people, and his legacy as a just and wise king endured for many years. He could accomplish his goals and have a happy life because he had mastered the discipline of setting priorities and maintaining focus.

Taking responsibility for yourself: It's critical to accept responsibility for your choices and actions and for the progress—or lack thereof—you are making towards your objectives. This entails scheduling frequent check-ins, monitoring your development, and being truthful about your accomplishments and shortcomings.

Accountability Is Essential for Development

Being responsible for your actions is a crucial part of developing yourself. It entails accepting accountability for the results of your choices, actions, behavior, and those acts themselves.

Being accountable entails accepting responsibility for your decisions and the results they produce and the ability to influence how you act and how others are affected. It also entails accepting responsibility for your errors, being open to making corrections when needed, and being honest with yourself and others.

Building credibility and trust with others is one of the main advantages of holding oneself accountable. It demonstrates your dependability, reliability, and trustworthiness when you accept accountability for your deeds and own up to your mistakes. Stronger relationships and more prospects for success in your personal and professional life can result from this.

Reaching your goals is another advantage of keeping oneself accountable. It is simpler to recognize the areas of your life that require development and to take the required action to bring about positive changes when you accept accountability for your actions. Happiness and a quicker and more effective completion of your goals.

Clearly defining your objectives and creating a strategy to reach them can help you keep yourself accountable. This will support you in maintaining motivation and focus as you move closer to your goal. It's crucial to be truthful with yourself about your development and to own up to any mistakes or setbacks you have along the road.

The capacity to evaluate your actions and choices and pinpoint areas for growth is a crucial component of holding oneself responsible. This can be accomplished by journaling, introspection, or asking for input from others. Being receptive to constructive criticism and maintaining an open mind are crucial because they can assist you in identifying areas of your life that require development and making positive adjustments.

Ultimately, it's critical to act and implement the required adjustments in order to better oneself. This could entail making new habits, gaining new abilities, or establishing new goals. It's critical to maintain your commitment to your goals and to remain persistent in the face of setbacks or hurdles.

In summary, one of the most important components of personal development is learning to hold oneself accountable. It entails accepting accountability for the results of your choices, actions, behavior, and those acts themselves. You may accomplish your goals, better yourself, and reach your full potential by holding yourself accountable. You can also gain the respect and credibility of others. Therefore, you must live an accountable lifestyle.

A little child named Jack once lived in a tiny village. Jack was a cheerful, joyous boy who enjoyed playing and discovering his surroundings. He had an insatiable curiosity and was always willing to explore new things.

Jack's father, a knowledgeable and well-respected village elder, once sat him down and had a serious conversation with him. "Jack, you have a lot of potential, but you need to learn to own up to your mistakes and hold yourself accountable for the consequences of your actions." You won't be able to reach your full potential and develop into the greatest version of yourself until then."

Even though Jack didn't understand what his father was saying, he decided to try to grasp what it meant to hold himself accountable. He started to become aware of the effects of his activities on other people. He began to own up to his errors and show that he was prepared to adjust when needed.

As Jack became older, he discovered numerous advantages to responsibility for himself. In addition to achieving his objectives more rapidly and effectively, he was able to gain the respect and credibility of others. Additionally, he discovered that he could evaluate his actions and choices and pinpoint areas where he needed to grow.

One day, Jack encountered a challenging situation. The crops in the village were failing due to the terrible drought. Jack decided to act after realizing that something needed to be done to preserve the community. After organizing the locals, they devised a scheme to construct a dam and establish a reservoir to store water.

Jack oversaw the reservoir and dam building, and he put much effort into ensuring the project was finished on schedule and on budget. Jack and the locals finished the project and saved the community despite numerous challenges and disappointments.

Creating the Conditions for Success: Explicit Expressions

Clear communication is essential for effective delegating. Ensure that the parameters, goals, and expectations are clear before handing over an assignment. Set the scene, state your objectives, and provide any resources or assistance that you may need. This clarity removes any uncertainty that can cause mistakes in addition to creating the conditions for success.

Observation and Guidance: The Significance of Persistence

Detachment is not the same as delegation. Regular check-ins and progress reports are crucial to ensure that activities are being completed on time. Consider it a journey of mentorship. Staying involved, providing direction, and resolving any obstacles helps to foster the development of the task and the person completing it.

Promoting a Culture That Accepts Delegation

Delegation is a culture that may spread throughout an entire team or organization; it's not just something that leaders do. An atmosphere conducive to delegation can be created by promoting an open discussion regarding delegation, cultivating a growth mentality, and acknowledging accomplishments. When everyone recognizes the need for delegation, work is distributed wisely, resulting in success as a group.

From Supervisor to Conductor

When you become skilled at assigning, you become more than just a taskmaster—you become an orchestra conductor. Your time management canvas turns into an amazing work of empowerment, teamwork, and efficiency. Your assigned tasks thrive in the capable hands that handle them, allowing you to concentrate on the higher-level strategic thinking that advances your objectives.

The Significance of Ongoing Education

Improving your time management abilities requires you to reflect on your past experiences and look for areas in which you can develop. Constant learning and development are the colorful threads that bind the complex picture of time management. Your path to ideal time management necessitates ongoing development, self-awareness, and a readiness to adjust, just as a painter and a musician practice their craft.

The Influence of Introspection: Examining Oneself

The foundation of personal development and improvement is self-reflection. It's looking in the mirror at your past experiences and deeds to gather perspective, draw conclusions, and make wise decisions. You build the groundwork for better time management by evaluating your accomplishments, difficulties, and opportunities for development.

Opening the Feedback Loop: Gaining Valuable Knowledge

Consider your experience with time management as a canvas, with comments serving as the rich palette of colors that enhance it. Getting input on your time management techniques from mentors, coworkers, and even yourself might provide you with new insights. You may improve upon your approach, eliminate inefficiencies, and leverage your abilities with the support of insightful critique and constructive feedback.

Accepting Adaptability: Using a Flexible Approach

Learning time management skills is a dynamic process rather than a static route. Accepting flexibility entails open-mindedness to new techniques, strategies, and resources that fit your changing requirements. Your time management strategies must adapt to new situations and technological advancements to remain effective.

Using Lifelong Learning to Promote Growth

See every day as a new chapter filled with lessons waiting to be discovered in the book of your personal development. Developing an insatiable curiosity in learning and progress propels you to master time management. Look for books, conferences, workshops, and internet resources that provide new viewpoints, tactics, and ideas. Your time management symphony gets more and more refined as you learn.

The Growth Mindset: Accepting Difficulties

The development attitude, or the unwavering conviction that obstacles are opportunities in disguise, is the cornerstone of any time management endeavor. Accept setbacks as stepping stones towards growth rather than something to fear. Every experience you have, whether taking on a challenging endeavor, running into unforeseen problems, or venturing into an unfamiliar area, helps you grow.

Building Resilience: Rebounding More Powerfully

Resilience is your defense against the storms of setbacks, just like a tree bends and sways with the wind but never breaks. Resilience equips you with the knowledge gained from experience to overcome obstacles and turnbacks with strength. This perseverance helps you maintain momentum and hone your time management skills.

Your Continual Path: A Growing Tapestry

Recall that improving your time management abilities evolves. Every instance of introspection, criticism, flexibility, and education adds a new layer to your work of art. Your time management skills improve, your goals become more reachable, and your impact deepens with each challenge you take on and the experience you harness.

Proactive Techniques for Time Management

Often, time management feels reactive. Yes, we do have objectives. Even better, they're SMART! However, despite our preparation, an unforeseen event took up to two hours. This may force you to make a lot of difficult decisions. It doesn't have to be this way, though. We can make plans if we anticipate a specific amount of crises. In Leigh's definition from 2023, Setting objectives, prioritizing work, and allocating resources are all part of proactive time management. It places a strong emphasis on managing your time and making deliberate decisions in order to accomplish goals.

But even with incomplete knowledge, we may create reasonable timetables in advance. Generally speaking, our work can be viewed as routines similar to those we discussed in our research on habit formation. Sequences that result in the intended result. Unlike with these routines, the result will be marginally different every time. For instance, quarterly reports would show different expenses if you were in charge of your region's accounting records. However, the procedure you would employ to complete them would be the same. Profit from these trends! They frequently take the same amount of time to finish. You can discover time pockets you weren't previously aware of if you combine this with your prior understanding of time blocking. Your productivity could skyrocket if you use these effectively!

Likewise, chances are you can schedule obligations in advance. In this statement, I refer to both personal and professional encounters. Make your plans well in advance rather than on the spur of the moment. Assume Fatima enjoys going out to eat once a month or so with her pals. But nowadays, they organize things a lot. This causes them to have two issues. As Fatima remembers, the planning day gets busy to start with. Not only is it stressful, but it's hard to know who will show up. Many of them skipped a few evenings, primarily because they were too busy to make the food. Fatima decides to schedule the following dinner a month in advance after seeing a problem. She calls the group together, and they decide when everyone's schedules are free. This even allows her enough time to get a reservation at their preferred cafe, ensuring a decent table. She has not only spared herself needless anxiety, but she has also improved her leadership abilities.

If you take a moment to reflect, you can discover that identical solutions are frequently needed for common emergencies. Using the Pareto Principle, it makes sense that most issues respond similarly to various approaches. As a result, we can create time blocks the size of these solutions even when we are unsure of what lies ahead. We have enough time to handle problems, even if they don't materialize. You must prevent this from turning into a major anxiety attack. Keep your composure while you strategize. I suggest box breathing again if you start to feel anxious. It's a powerful way to address these unhelpful emotions.

There will also be instances where peculiar issues arise. Suppose Brian decided to change the budgetary allotment to his department. Everything was going well, with a notable improvement in marketing KPIs. Yet, client satisfaction started to decline a few days following deployment. Thankfully, Brian uses a structure similar to the one we previously covered. He had conjectured about a few potential issues that his solution might raise. This indicated that he had thought about how it would affect consumer pleasure. He was, therefore, able to take more immediate action by the time it occurred.

Lastly, there are a few instances where the issue is completely unanticipated. For instance, I began my career as an accounting assistant at a national computer business. My manager summoned our team to an urgent meeting, but there was nothing on the agenda. Usually, she would meticulously prepare schedules for these events, but this time was different. I arrived with my teammates. She had submitted her resignation and was checking in to ensure everything would continue as usual once she left for a new position. Not a single person in the room had anticipated this. In these out-of-the-ordinary situations, trust your instincts and flexibility. Be proactive in your methodical approach, just as you were with problem-solving. Since you might not be able to prepare for them, systematic thinking might provide a means of streamlining the circumstances.

The most potent use of proactive time management may be one final application. Growing is best achieved by being proactive. It provides you with much leverage to make personal actions more realistic, as Fatima's example demonstrated. This also holds for more somber objectives. For instance, one of my current goals is to finish a 10k marathon before the end of the year. To get here, I've used a few different tools. First, I've routinely blocked out time in my calendar for practicing. I could barely go for a km or so before giving up. However, I've had a goal to meet every month. In addition, I've looked into forums and asked some friends and colleagues to participate in this challenge with me. It brings another level of accountability but brings us all a bit closer. As a last resort, I decided to get new tennis shoes, especially for marathoning. It's difficult to measure how much better these are than formal loafers.

However, don't let anyone fool you into believing it's been an easy ride. Even though I took many steps to be successful, I failed in May. I was around 400 meters shy of the milestone. But I did what I've always advised: I worked on being compassionate to myself. I've been able to run eight kilometers in a single session because of this. In addition, I took part in two lesser tournaments. You can accomplish your goals more consistently than you might think if you apply comparable concepts.

These guidelines also apply to professional development. On the other hand, you might need to go to events and network instead of running. Alternatively, sign up for classes that will increase your value. Don't be hesitant to treat yourself financially. The one investment you can always count on is yourself. In order to further your knowledge of project management, you might consider obtaining an official certification. In due course, it will pay for itself.

Additionally, utilize internal resources to the fullest. Many businesses provide their staff with growth programs. Certain ones, like technical training and entrepreneurship programs, are rather obvious. Some might not be as clear-cut. For instance, make a proactive request for a project or assignment that piques your interest! Try to learn from a potential mentor if you sincerely regard their abilities. In some extremely lucky circumstances, this can become a mentoring!

The majority of our book's focus has been on offices. Time management is helpful in a lot more situations, though. For example, a large number of the research that I consulted are dependent on students. I advise you to read the next chapter even if the lives it describes don't define you. It's amazing how much information written from various perspectives can teach us. Several of my musician colleagues say that gamelan music from Java has made them aware of musical possibilities they would not have otherwise thought of. Thus, be open-minded. However, the next chapter is specifically for you, whether you are studying, taking care of your kids, or perhaps having the guts to launch your own business. I hope that having techniques tailored to your condition in your daily life is beneficial.

Chapter 8: Managing Your Time in Particular Situations

There is a small PR issue with time management. Although it's a skill that can be used anywhere, at first glance, it appears stiff. Stereotypes support this idea even more. Protagonists are not typically those who are very well-organized. They aren't considered to be as "interesting" by Hollywood. Despite the obvious irony, these things discourage many people who could gain from studying time management. It almost seems like a highly valued company trade secret. This chapter is mostly intended for those who don't fit the mold of the nine-to-five workers or have extra responsibilities that make time management appear unmanageable. Although some individuals belong to every group I refer to, we'll discuss the advice separately.

Naturally, apply advice from all of these scenarios if they apply to your life! Let's start with academics and time management.

9- Establishing a Culture of Time Management

How to Promote an Effective and Productive Work Environment.

Establishing a culture of time management is essential to having an effective and productive workplace. In this chapter, we'll look at the tactics business owners can employ to instill a time management culture in their companies.

1. Once more! Set an example for others.

When managing their time well, business owners need to set an example. Business owners can inspire their team members to adopt effective time management practices by setting an example. This entails being punctual, fulfilling obligations, and exhibiting a dedication to efficiency.

2. Express Your Expectations

In order to create a culture of time management, communication must be clear. Owners of businesses need to let their staff members know what is expected of them in terms of time management. This entails establishing deadlines, giving precise directions, and describing the repercussions of missing deadlines.

3. Offer Assistance and Resources

Owners of businesses should give their staff members the tools and encouragement they require to manage their time efficiently. This entails giving people access to time management software and tools, training them in time management skills, and providing help and direction when required.

4. Promote Teamwork

An integral part of a culture focused on time management is collaboration. When team members collaborate, they can assign tasks to one another in a priority list and hold one another responsible for completing tasks by the deadline. Company owners should promote Teamwork by fostering a culture of cooperation and giving employees chances to work together.

5. Acknowledge and Honour Productivity

Establishing a time management culture can be greatly aided by rewarding and recognizing productivity. Owners of businesses should recognize team members who regularly fulfill deadlines, exhibit effective time management techniques, and increase the company's overall productivity. This can be accomplished through rewards like bonuses, promotions, or other recognition.

6. Constantly Assess and Enhance

Creating a culture of time management takes time. Owners of businesses must constantly assess how well their staff members manage their time and seek out opportunities for improvement. This could entail adjusting deadlines, offering more resources or assistance, or implementing new time management techniques.

Actual Cases

Here are a few actual instances of how entrepreneurs have created a time management culture within their companies:

• A marketing agency recognizes and rewards productivity by offering bonuses for meeting deadlines and allowing team members to present their work to clients. A software development company holds weekly team meetings, gives access to Asana for task management, and offers training on time management techniques.

- Strict production schedules, time tracking tools, and team member accountability for meeting deadlines are ways a manufacturing company sets clear expectations for time management.

Final Thoughts

Establishing a culture of time management is crucial to having an effective and productive workplace. Business owners can encourage a time management culture within their organizations by setting a good example, setting clear expectations, communicating those expectations, offering resources and support, encouraging collaboration, recognizing and rewarding productivity, and continuously monitoring and improving. Recall that creating a time management culture within an organization is a continuous process that necessitates the involvement and dedication of all members.

4. Not Monitoring Your Time

You can't improve your time management strategies and techniques if you don't track your time. Time tracking may seem like a laborious task, but if you make it a habit, you'll find that it reveals interesting patterns and insights. One can adopt a more strategic approach to managing their time by calculating the number of hours that emails, phone calls, and other distractions consume.

Time management advice.

● Select the time tracking instrument that works best for you, such as a stopwatch timer, desktop time tracker, smartphone app, or browser extension.

● Examine time monitoring applications. Select the device that satisfies your requirements without overburdening you with features or an intricate UI.

● Regularly assess your performance. Record time against tasks using Excel sheets, Google Sheets, timesheet apps, or time trackers with project management tools. You may then use your time logs to create reports.

5. Dim Vision

First, if you don't know where you want to go, there's no reason to become an expert time manager. You must first generate greater direction and meaning if the duties and obligations you wish to handle with more elegance and expertise don't motivate you. You won't be able to achieve your goals or feel motivated to keep going if you don't have a clear vision.

Time management advice: ● Take a broad perspective. Consider how the tasks at hand further your professional or personal objectives. Keep your eyes on the prize; this will motivate and inspire you to keep going. Never lose sight of your vision, even if you have to adjust it.

Decide who is wasting time. Most management issues arise from devoting excessive time to activities that don't advance and produce results. Make sure you devote your time to worthwhile endeavors and assignments.

● Make an emergency plan. It's always possible that events won't go as planned. To handle risks and issues gracefully, consider best- and worst-case situations and have "Plan B" and "Plan C" ready.

6. Refusing to Consider Tomorrow

Those who do remarkable things in life are usually visionaries. They must think strategically and develop short-term objectives that move them closer to their goals to turn their visions into reality. When you plan for Tomorrow, you'll be more organized for what lies ahead and inspired to put in the daily work necessary to achieve your goals.

Here are some time management pointers: ● Improve your awareness and flexibility. Consider how the time and energy you put in today will help you achieve your goals and make Tomorrow a reality (e.g., how will the project tasks from today affect the tasks from next week?). Make adjustments to your plans as conditions change.

● Regularly assess your progress. Divide your projects into doable tasks and monitor their development. To monitor your progress, use reports, charts, and progress bars.

● Think about the seven-minute rule. Plan your day for seven minutes in the morning, and evaluate and create a plan for Tomorrow's activities seven minutes before bed.

● Take lessons from your previous work. Set deadlines, estimate your work, and monitor your progress towards them. If you need more competition, evaluate your performance after completing the assignment, see any trends, and turn it into a game to improve your performance the next time.

7. Insufficient Periodic Review of Time Management

Periodically reviewing your performance is important, whether you're working towards personal objectives or increasing productivity at work. If you utilize time-tracking software, you may find productivity trends, modify your strategy, and make even more efficient use of your time by analyzing your time logs and creating reports. To obtain a broad overview of your work, examine your daily and weekly performance and your monthly and half-year reports.

Tips for managing your time: ● Steer clear of the sunk cost fallacy, which involves spending excessive time on low-value and ineffective tasks. When you find that the time you spend on your present task is more than you can manage, take a step back and assess how important the result is and how it will impact your progress.

● View things from a future time frame. Consider how your current activity will benefit or hinder your project, your upcoming tasks for next week, and your future actions.

● Consistently check your schedule. Review your daily schedule for five minutes at the beginning of the day. Review your progress and the outstanding tasks quickly in the middle of the day. Have a five-minute performance review to round off your day.

● Create a personal development plan and record your objectives, strategies, and necessary abilities. Consistently assess your progress to ensure that you remain on course.

8. Being Unable to Handle Stress

Time management and stress reduction frequently go hand in hand. You'll probably feel stressed if you put off doing the task at hand until the last minute, don't prepare ahead, and don't prioritize. While not all Stress is harmful, prolonged Stress affects health. Let's explore some effective stress management techniques for you.

Time management advice: ● Recognise your sources of Stress. For a few weeks, try journaling to capture your thoughts, feelings, reactions, and stressors. Review your notes to look for trends and research further coping mechanisms for Stress.

● Create sensible reactions. While stress-relieving junk food and drink may seem like a good idea, consider healthier options like yoga, meditation, exercise, hobbies, and restful sleep.

Establish limits. Keep to your work schedule and leave work at work, whether from home or the office. After work, try not to think about work, respond to emails, silence corporate chats, or check other work-related notifications on your smartphone.

9. Not Using Attention Control Techniques

It's a fact that every one of us has a full day and that "managing time" does not exist. We can control our attention and focus, which is fantastic news. In the end, attention management is the capacity to identify your mental state and deliberately change it to benefit you the most. While we won't get into specifics here, we will provide you with some suggestions on how to focus on your task.

Time-management advice:

Take charge of your surroundings. Tell people you're trying to focus by turning on headphones, closing the door, or changing your chat status to "Don't disturb." Do whatever is acceptable for the circumstances.

Examine your tendencies to divert focus. When working from home, some of us prefer to have the sound of the TV on in the background, and most of us can't help but be tempted to check our notifications and respond to messages as soon as possible. To improve your focus and attention span, identify and evaluate your unhealthy time management practices and create a more beneficial schedule.

- Workout and mindfulness. Exercise enhances mental acuity, memory, and concentration. A study found that even a few weeks of meditation can improve memory and focus and minimize daydreaming.

10. Taking Care of Everything Alone

Whether you work for a company, are self-employed, or are an employee, you cannot accomplish everything alone. Humans all have a finite amount of energy and a day that lasts 24 hours. Thus, overexerting ourselves increases the likelihood that we will experience Stress, become less productive, and produce subpar work.

Time-management advice:

● Contract out. If you are self-employed or a business owner, consider outsourcing some of your work. For instance, think about hiring the services of accounting agencies if the accounting routine takes up a lot of your time. Considering the opportunity costs, you can discover that investing time and energy is more important for your success than financial resources.

● Make your routines automated. As a project manager, you might have to monitor the status of your work, the performance of your team, and invoicing and financial issues. Most of this labor can be completed by time tracking software; therefore, once more, weigh the opportunity costs before deciding to buy it. Over time, automated processes will save you weeks of work.

- Assign. Assume you oversee a marketing team and are overburdened with administrative duties, job interviews, reports, and meetings. Think about assigning a report-building assignment to one of your team members who is the most dependable and meticulous. In this manner, you'll have more time to work on projects that directly involve you, and they'll pick up some new abilities and be ready to support you later.

Chapter 21: Retirement Savings

Even though retirement may seem far off, it's crucial to begin saving and planning now. Since time is money, the earlier you start saving, the more time you have. This chapter will examine the phases involved in retirement savings and offer advice and anecdotes to assist with future planning.

Step 1: Determine Your Needs

Identifying your needs is the first step in saving for retirement. Think about the kind of retirement you want and the associated costs. Are you planning to travel? Pursuing interests as a hobby? Relocating to a new place? It's critical to comprehend your retirement objectives and the related expenses.

Tip: Based on your intended retirement age, current age, and lifestyle objectives, use retirement calculators to estimate how much you need to save for retirement. You can use these calculators to determine how much annual savings you'll need to meet your retirement objectives.

Story: John and Mary's retirement was well-defined in their minds. In addition to seeing the world, they want to spend time with their grandchildren. Their anticipated savings needed to support their retirement was $1.5 million. Using a retirement calculator, they calculated that to attain their target, they would need to save $30,000 a year for the following 20 years.

Step 2: Begin Saving Earlier

It's best to begin retirement savings as early as possible. You will need to save more money annually to meet your retirement goals the longer you put off starting to save. Time is money. It's critical to begin saving as soon as possible, even if you can only manage a modest monthly sum.

IRAs should be utilized. By allowing you to save money before taxes, raise your savings. Furthermore, many companies match employee contributions, which helps expedite reaching your retirement objectives.

Narrative: Sarah's retirement savings began when she took her first job. Even though initially she could only save $50 a month, she knew that time would be on her side. She grew her funds and benefited from her employer's matching contributions. She had amassed a sizeable retirement fund by the time she retired.

Companies need to be aware of these distinctions and establish a well-balanced workplace that meets the requirements of both regular and remote workers.

Difficulties Businesses Face When Embracing Remote Work

Companies are just as different as their people. Organizational cultures, structures, or other limitations may make it more difficult for a business to adopt remote work practices. Typical difficulties include the following:

Lack of faith in staff: Organisations prioritizing stringent supervision and micromanagement may find it difficult to put their faith in staff members to perform well and autonomously in a remote environment.

Roles that are not well defined: It may be difficult for businesses with overlapping or ambiguous job responsibilities to switch to remote work since employees may need assistance handling several tasks digitally.

Profit-driven mentality: Even if remote work arrangements could help their workforce, companies that prioritize earnings more than their employees' welfare may be reluctant to invest.

Insufficient communication infrastructure: Organisations with weak communication systems could be reluctant to accept remote work because they fear the expenses and time needed to change their current configuration.

Blame-based culture: Working remotely can be especially difficult in companies where staff members deflect blame and shirk accountability, which lowers output and raises expenses.

Long-term leases on office space: Rather than investing in remote work arrangements, companies with long-term office leases may decide to keep using their office space.

Problems with middle management: Remote employment can upset established power structures, resulting in disputes between middle- and lower-level staff members. In a remote work environment, managers who feel less powerful could want assistance staying motivated and productive.

Businesses may want to implement a hybrid work style that blends remote and in-person labor. Employee preferences and productivity requirements are met while allowing them to maintain a work-life balance. To learn more about the requirements and preferences of their workforce, employers can communicate directly with employees or use surveys to get input.

Ultimately, a smooth transition to remote work depends on comprehending and meeting the organization's and its workers' particular demands. By encouraging open communication and flexibility, employers may establish a work atmosphere that is inclusive, balanced, and supportive of traditional and remote employees.

Taking Adjacent Actions

As well as the benefits and downsides for employers and employees while determining the best work arrangement for your company. Recall that you don't have to coerce your staff to work only from home or in an office. As a manager or business owner, it is your responsibility to determine if remote work or in-office work is more productive for your company.

Analyze the expenses and advantages for the business and the staff.

Find out whether employees would prefer to work in-person or remotely.

To accommodate both forms of employment, consider providing hybrid work arrangements.

Make sure the decisions you make will help the business and its employees.

Thinking Back on Problems and Solutions

Note all the personal and business issues that could arise in a remote team environment to better comprehend the difficulties associated with working remotely and develop workable solutions. Next, consider the approaches and systems to deal with these problems.

Which business or personal matters need your attention?

Which systems should be designed or implemented to solve the issues you identified during your brainstorming session?

Transcending Stereotypes and Shifting Attitudes

Overcoming established mental patterns and preexisting stigmas is frequently necessary to adjust to remote employment. Take into account the following actions to make this move easier:

Promote open communication by fostering an inclusive and transparent culture that allows staff members to express their ideas and concerns.

Give employees access to resources and training to assist them in becoming more proficient at working remotely and to help them adjust to new work practices.

Tell success stories: Provide uplifting instances of remote work that your company has implemented, emphasizing the advantages and productivity it may provide.

Dispel myths: Be proactive in dispelling rumors or misconceptions about remote work and how it affects output and employee satisfaction.

Stress the value of a healthy work-life balance. Encourage staff members to draw boundaries between their personal and work lives. Even when working remotely.

Provide direction and purpose to remote workers by setting explicit expectations and goals that are both clear and specific.

Your company and its employees will benefit from a more flexible and adaptive work environment if these issues are addressed and workable solutions are implemented. Successful people must embrace change and cultivate a growth attitude as the workplace changes.

Chapter 4: How Can You Put These Ideas and Techniques Into Your Everyday Life? What Are Some Useful Hints and Techniques?

This chapter will teach you:

● A few useful tidbits and shortcuts to help you incorporate the ideas and tactics from Chapter 3 into your everyday activities.

● How to select the finest advice and shortcuts based on your character, tastes, or circumstances.

● How to assess the efficacy of these tricks and ideas and change accordingly.

What Are Some Useful Hints and Techniques for Putting These Ideas and Approaches Into Your Everyday Life?

There are tonnes of tricks and pointers that will help you incorporate the ideas and methods from Chapter 3 into your everyday life. Not all of them might be appropriate for you or your circumstances. As a result, you must experiment to see what suits you the best.

Here are a few of the most well-liked and practical hints and techniques you might use:

● Creating SMART goals: You can use the SMART acronym as a reference when creating SMART goals. Ask yourself if each goal is specific. Can you measure it? Is it feasible to achieve? Does it Matter? Is there a time limit? You can also record your goals and monitor your progress using a goal-setting worksheet or template. You can also utilize a goal-setting tool or software to establish alerts, notifications, or reminders for your goals.

● Setting task priorities: There are several techniques you can use to set task priorities, including the Eisenhower Method, the Priority Matrix, and the ABCD analysis. As part of the ABCD analysis, tasks are ranked from A to D based on urgency and importance. The jobs in A are the most crucial and urgent, while the duties in B, C, and D are neither crucial nor urgent, important nor urgent, and urgent but unimportant. Using the Priority Matrix, your tasks are divided. Tasks in Quadrant 1 are both urgent and significant; tasks in Quadrant 2 are significant but not urgent; tasks in Quadrant 3 are urgent but not significant; and tasks in Quadrant 4 are neither significant nor urgent. For every task, ask yourself two questions using the Eisenhower Method: Is it important?

Is it critical? You can choose to complete it now, later, assign it to someone else, or delete it based on your responses.

● Planning ahead: You can utilize various tools, including calendars, schedules, action plans, checklists, and more, to prepare ahead. A calendar helps you keep track of the dates and times of your meetings and events. One tool that helps you see the order and length of your chores or activities is a timetable. Objectives are action plans that outline the necessary steps and resources. A checklist is a tool that helps you keep track of the tasks or things you need to finish or double-check. For planning, you can utilize digital or paper-based methods. Using a planning app or program, you can also make, modify, and distribute your plans.

● Delegating and outsourcing: There are various methods you can use to assign and outsource work, including hiring agencies, contractors, or freelancers; using online platforms or services; or asking coworkers, family, or friends for assistance. Use services like Upwork, Fiverr, or Freelancer to find freelancers, contractors, or agencies. You may post project information, budget, and deadlines there and get bids from people who meet the qualifications. You can use online platforms or services like TaskRabbit, Zaarly, or Fancy Hands, where you can pay an hourly rate or a fixed cost for various jobs like deliveries, cleaning, and errands. You can utilize technologies like email, phone, text, or social media to ask for help from coworkers, family, or friends. You can use these channels to explain your assignment, its reasons, and your expectations. You can also ask for their availability, interest, or expertise.

● Batching and automating: You can use many methods, such as apps, software, tools, templates, scripts, or workflows, as well as rules, alerts, or reminders, to batch and automate jobs. Programs like Zapier, IFTTT, or Automate.io allow you to connect several apps or services and build automatic processes or activities. These programs can be used to use apps, software, or tools. For instance, you may use Zapier to automatically send emails to your clients when they purchase from your website.

● You can use apps like Google Docs, Microsoft Word, or Evernote to create and save documents or notes that you can reuse or change for different jobs to construct templates, scripts, or workflows. For instance, you can make a template for your reports or invoices using Google Docs. You can construct and apply rules or filters to your emails or events using Gmail, Outlook, or Calendar to set up rules, alerts, or reminders. Gmail allows you to automatically archive or remove, for instance.

● Distraction Elimination: There are several methods to reduce distractions, including turning off calls, messages, and notifications; closing tabs, windows, or apps that aren't needed; using headphones, earplugs, or noise-canceling devices; organizing your workspace, desk, or surroundings; and establishing boundaries with people. You can utilize settings like Do Not Disturb mode on your computer or phone to turn off calls, messages, and notifications. By doing this, you may stop any warnings from appearing on your screen and silence all of the sounds and vibrations coming from your device. Additionally, you can configure this mode to accept specified calls or messages from particular contacts.

● You can use browser extensions like OneTab, Tab Wrangler, or StayFocusd to close tabs, windows, or apps that aren't needed. These will assist you in minimizing the number of tabs, windows, or open applications at any given time and keep you from becoming sidetracked by unrelated information or websites.

● You can also impose restrictions, time limitations, or blocks on particular websites or applications that you find bothersome. In order to assist you in decompressing or reenergizing, you can also listen to music, podcasts, or white noise.

● You can apply techniques like the 5S system, the KonMari method, or the minimalist approach to your physical area to declutter your desk, workspace, or surroundings. These will assist you in simplifying, organizing, and clearing out your workspace to make it more suitable for working in.

Additionally, you can incorporate plants, artwork, or lighting to elevate your mood or spark your creativity.

● You can also request assistance or cooperation from others by letting them know about your availability, expectations, or preferences.

Chapter 6: Combining Rest Periods with Free Time

The Value of Rest Periods in Time Management

We face a maze of activities, initiatives, and objectives in our daily lives, which frequently push us over the edge into burnout. Continuous activity may appear beneficial in the short run. However, it can harm our mental and physical well-being and our capacity for time management in the long run. This is where breaks play a very important role.

First of all, our brains require breaks. The cognitive functions of labor, study, and other mental tasks require significant energy from our brains. This level of energy use cannot be sustained over time. As a result, breaks enable our brains to regenerate, enabling us to continue operating at a high level all day. Breaks provide an additional chance for information processing and consolidation. Your brain can reorder and retain what you have learned or experienced during these times, enhancing memory retention and fostering creativity. You can see things differently and devise creative solutions to difficulties by pausing to contemplate. Furthermore, taking pauses is a great way to manage stress. Prolonged stress can impair our capacity to concentrate and finish things effectively and have detrimental effects on our health and general well-being. We can lower our stress levels and revitalize our bodies and minds by pausing and unwinding.

Breaks can also aid in preventing burnout. When we are mentally and physically worn out by chronic stress or work overload, we experience burnout. Decreased motivation, productivity, and life happiness may result from this. We may avoid this state by taking regular pauses, which enables us to remain highly motivated and dedicated to our work.

Taking breaks is essential for preserving our physical well-being. A large portion of the population spends their days in a sedentary position, which can result in heart disease, obesity, and diabetes, among other health issues. It can be helpful to reduce these hazards to take some time to get up, stretch, and walk around.

Even though breaks have many obvious advantages, many people struggle to fit them into their schedules. Breaks could be seen as a waste of time or an indication of sloth. However, this is untrue. A crucial component of efficient and long-term time management is taking breaks.

Regular and predictable breaks are crucial to include them in your routine. This might be as easy as walking after lunch or stretching every hour. Effective breaks don't have to be lengthy. Some research indicates frequent, brief breaks might be more advantageous than longer, less frequent ones.

Ensuring that your breaks are genuinely soothing is equally crucial. Steer clear of things like checking your email or the news that could make your day more stressful. Instead, consider rejuvenating and relaxing pursuits like reading, meditation, or enjoying nature.

To sum up, breaks are an important time management tool. They can assist you in maintaining a high degree of performance and enjoyment by enabling you to refuel, process information, lessen stress, avoid burnout, and preserve physical health. Thus, remember that you're investing long-term in your productivity the next time you are inclined to skip a break.

How to properly incorporate downtime and breaks

Without question, learning and mastering time management is an essential ability everyone should possess. But it's also critical to understand that scheduling enough downtime and leisure time into our schedules is necessary to sustain our mental and physical well-being. In this section, we'll talk about how to successfully incorporate these necessary elements into our daily lives.

Let's first discuss the significance of breaks and leisure time. The human brain is not always made to operate at a high level of focus. Rest times are necessary for information processing and consolidation, idea generation, and preventing mental exhaustion. Additionally, leisure time allows us to unwind, enjoy ourselves, and refuel for impending activities.

Now, how can we successfully integrate these components into our routine?

1. Planning and scheduling breaks: Rather than being an afterthought, we should prioritize including breaks into our daily schedules. We have to schedule our breaks in the same way that we schedule our commitments and tasks. For instance, the Pomodoro approach recommends working for 25 minutes, followed by a 5-minute rest. Maintaining

a balance between work and relaxation periods lowers the likelihood of mental fatigue and aids in concentration.

2. Diversification of breaks: Different breaks have different purposes. Some can be brief and only enable us to put down the screen, while others might be longer and let us partake in an activity for fun. Taking varied breaks throughout the day can help us stay mentally stimulated and improve productivity.

3. Activities that promote relaxation and renewal: We mustn't spend all our leisure time watching TV or browsing the Internet. Active pastimes like reading, painting, playing an instrument, and playing sports might be more gratifying and revitalizing. These

pursuits give us a break from our professional responsibilities and let us explore our hobbies and interests.

4. Digital Downtime: We are continuously inundated with information and pleas for our attention in this digital age. We must, therefore, schedule a period of digital isolation during our free time. This is shutting off our electronics at specific times to prevent distractions and allow our thoughts to relax.

5. Respect for breaks and free time: Lastly, and maybe most crucially, we must honor our free and rest periods. This implies that we must commit to refrain from working during the break or time off we have arranged. We can

preserve a healthy work-life balance because of this distinct division between work and leisure time.

Recall that integrating breaks and downtime efficiently does not equate to working fewer hours. It indicates that you're operating more strategically and understanding how crucial it is to recover physically and mentally to continue operating at your best. Ultimately, time management is about striking a balance that lets you work as hard as possible while caring for your health. It's not just about packing every minute with tasks.

2.3 Forming an Action Schedule

After defining your SMART goals, the next stage is to draft an action plan to guide you toward achieving them. An action plan is a thorough list of the actions and steps you must take to accomplish your goals. Creating an action plan can help you stay motivated, focused, and organized as you work towards your goals. This is how to draft a successful action plan:

1. Break your objective into smaller, more doable activities or benchmarks. This facilitates achieving the objective and aids in your consistent advancement. If your objective is to complete a marathon in six months, you may divide it into smaller goals like running a longer distance each week, picking up a faster pace, or entering shorter races.

2. Set task priorities: Decide which tasks are most crucial or urgent, then order them in that order. This might assist you in concentrating on the activities that will most significantly affect how close you are to achieving your objective.

3. Establish deadlines: Give each task or milestone a deadline to foster a sense of urgency and help you stay on course. Ensure your deadlines are reasonable and doable, accounting for your time and other obligations.

4. Determine resources and support: Ascertain the tools, resources, or assistance required to finish each activity. Books, online classes, mentors, and specialized tools and equipment

may all fall under this category. By being aware of these resources beforehand, you can reduce obstacles and remain organized.

5. Progress should be regularly reviewed and tracked as you progress toward each goal or milestone. This might support you in maintaining your motivation and modifying your action plan as needed if you encounter difficulties.

6. Make necessary adjustments to your strategy: Be ready to change your action plan if anything comes up, if you find a better way to accomplish your goal, or if your circumstances change. Success requires both adaptability and flexibility.

7. Celebrate your successes: Give yourself a pat for your efforts as you finish tasks and reach milestones. This can support you in staying motivated and gaining momentum towards your objective.

Developing and adhering to a well-organized action plan can improve your chances of reaching your SMART objectives. As you work towards your goals, an action plan will help you keep organized and motivated by providing a clear roadmap.

2.4 Monitoring Your Development

It is essential to keep track of and monitor your progress to maintain your motivation and ensure you are moving in the right direction towards your objectives. You can pinpoint any improvement areas and modify your action plan by routinely assessing your progress. Here are some efficient methods for monitoring your development:

1. Use a notebook or planner: Jot down your daily or weekly goals, successes, and introspection. By doing this, you may evaluate your progress, stay organized, and learn what is and is not working.

2. Establish a visual tracking system: Make a chart, graph, or calendar that shows your progress and that you can alter as you finish tasks and reach milestones. This might give you a clear

picture of your development and inspire you.

3. Use digital tools and apps: Use apps and digital platforms like Trello, Asana, or Todoist, specially made for goal tracking. You may set reminders, keep track of your projects, and, if necessary, work with others using these tools.

4. Plan frequent check-ins: Decide on a frequency of once a week, twice a week, or once a month to examine your progress. Assess your progress towards your objectives throughout these check-ins, and modify your action plan as needed.

5. Consider your accomplishments: As you monitor your development, pause to consider and acknowledge your

achievements. This can increase your drive and support you in keeping an optimistic outlook.

6. Ask for feedback: If acceptable, discuss your development with a coach, mentor, friend, or family member who can offer insightful criticism and inspiration. They might also provide fresh insights or assist you in identifying possible areas for development.

7. Modify your objectives or action plan: Be ready to modify your goals or action plan based on your progress tracking. This could entail rearranging deadlines, distributing resources differently, or establishing new benchmarks.

A regular progress log will keep you motivated, engaged, and on course to meet your objectives. Make the most of your time and resources by combining these techniques.

Examining and Modifying Your Objectives

It's critical to regularly assess your goals as you progress toward them and make any required adjustments. This procedure can assist you in maintaining your moral compass, adjusting to new situations, and consistently increasing your productivity and time management. The following actions will assist you in reviewing and modifying your goals:

1. Evaluate your development: Analyze each goal's progress by contrasting it with the initial set of SMART criteria. Evaluate if your goals have been met and if not, pinpoint the causes of any obstacles or delays.

2. Evaluate your top priorities: Check if your priorities still reflect your values and long-term goals as you review your goals. Your priorities may vary as a result of personal development and life events. Therefore, it's critical to review them frequently.

3. Recognize barriers and difficulties: Identify obstacles impeding your efforts to reach your objectives. Consider if you can solve these problems with changes

to your action plan, more resources, or other people's help.

4. Adjust your goals as necessary: Determine whether any of your goals require revision in light of your thoughts and evaluations. This can entail modifying the goals' scope, duration, or particular objectives to better suit your priorities and present situation.

5. Revise your action plan: Make the necessary updates to your plan in light of any new difficulties or goals. This can entail setting new objectives, modifying due dates, or looking for more resources to assist you in overcoming challenges.

6. Create new objectives: As your initial goals are met or surpassed, create new ones that align with your long-term aims

and present priorities. Regularly setting and achieving new goals can help you keep pace and promote personal development.

7. Remain adaptive and flexible: Recognize that your priorities and goals may change over time, and be ready to modify your plans as necessary. Adopt a growth attitude and see chances for learning and improvement in changes and setbacks.

You must regularly evaluate and tweak your goals to keep your time management techniques productive and in line with your values and ambitions. You can stay motivated and focused and move closer to your goals by doing these things.

Regaining Focus with Digital Mindfulness Practices

Applying mindfulness to your digital life can overcome online distractions and reclaim your intention and attention.

Methodical technical testing

Consider your internet activities and establish goals before using any digital devices. This little break lessens reflexive aimless searching and increases mindfulness.

Online mindfulness training

Engage in digital mindfulness meditation, using your increased presence and awareness to connect with digital content. This activity enhances your capacity to pay attention and block out distractions.

In brief

Understanding the psychological underpinnings of procrastination in the digital age is essential to navigating the maze of online distractions. You may reclaim control over your attention and lessen the negative effects of online distractions by implementing a digital detox, practicing mindful consumption, and using time-tracking applications. Utilizing digital wellness features' tools and methods for setting up a meaningful digital workspace and engaging with technology mindfully, you may take advantage of the advantages of the digital age without becoming sidetracked by it. By including these techniques in your daily routine, you may create a balanced, goal-directed approach to digital connection that encourages a more productive and satisfying existence. Building on these ideas, the upcoming chapters will provide sophisticated strategies for conquering procrastination in various scenarios and contexts, enabling you to succeed in your pursuits and careers.

Goals for Action in Chapter Ten: A Successful Habit Cultivation Technique

Establishing objectives is a crucial first step in professional and personal development, but putting them into practice frequently requires overcoming procrastination's inertia. This gap is filled by developing productive habits that translate intentions into regular action. This chapter looks at practical methods for making goals into habits. It also offers advice on changing behavior, adopting new habits, and creating successful habits that increase productivity.

The Foundations of Behavior Change: The Power of Habit

Our daily lives are shaped by automatic behaviors known as habits. Understanding the science underlying habit development enables you to proactively create habits that support your goal-achieving.

habit loop

Benchmarks, routines, and rewards define the basic cycle of habits. A cue triggers the behavior, is habitual, and is reinforced by a reward. It is essential to recognize and work with these elements in order to build habits.

stacking habits

"Habit stacking" is incorporating a new habit into an existing one. You can generate an environment that supports the development of new behaviors by employing an established habit as a signal.

Important Routines: Amplification of positive change

Key habits are those routines that cascade and influence other aspects of your life. Finding and keeping important habits can have a domino effect that increases output.

Work out

Frequent exercise is a basic habit that impacts many facets of life. Being physically active frequently enhances mental acuity, vitality, and general health, all of which enhance productivity.

Eating healthily: A factor in decision-making

Eating a balanced diet can help with self-control and decision-making, which can help with time management and work prioritizing, among other aspects of life.

Rule 21/90: Regularity in the development of habits

begins, and it takes 90 days to fully form. Maintaining a regular schedule throughout these times will encourage the formation of enduring habits that increase productivity.

First commitment (21 days): Habits must be continuously formed during the first 21 days. Even if it takes deliberate effort, incorporate that behavior into your daily routine throughout this period.

Extended integration (sixty-nine days)

Over the next ninety days, the new routine will be integrated and reinforced. You will feel less internal struggle as your behavior becomes habitual and a normal part of your day.

Habit Monitoring and Accountability: Long-Term Development

Keep tabs on your development and establish accountability systems to ensure your efforts to cultivate habits remain successful and constant.

Tracker of habits

Apps for tracking habits let you monitor your progress and maintain accountability for your objectives. Maintaining a visual record of your actions helps to reinforce the habit loop and shows you where you've come from.

dependable partner

Ask a buddy, mentor, or accountability partner to help you take responsibility for your actions. Frequent updates and subscriptions foster a community that motivates you to commit to developing productive habits.

The Influence of Small Routines Little actions have a large effect

Small, controllable behaviors known as micro-habits are the foundation for larger habits. Including micro-habits in your routine can help you make consistent progress and less resistance to change.

Two-minute limit

According to the two-minute rule, you should start any work that can be finished in two minutes. In order to keep you motivated, this micro-habit helps you avoid accumulating tiny jobs.

gradual advancement

You can advance gradually with micro-habits without feeling overwhelmed. You can lower your psychological barrier to starting and raise your chances of sticking with it by concentrating on little steps.

Method for Forming Habits: From objective to action

Deliberate tactics that address motivation, triggers, and consistency are needed to transform goals into productive habits. Intent to perform

Indicate your preferred routines and when and where they will be performed to create performance intent. This tactic links behavior to a particular situation, which improves habit performance.

Honors and Festivities

Reward the development of a habit by associating it with something positive. Honor your accomplishments and growth, no matter how minor, to help you link good feelings to actions.

Establish a Looping Habit: Reward, Routine, and Reflection

Creating a routine, choosing rewards, and monitoring your progress are all necessary steps in creating a habit loop.

Typical

Create a specific regimen or series of behaviors that help you form the desired habit. In your daily existence, repetition serves to encourage certain behaviors.

Reward

Find a reward that is related to the habit and has intrinsic satisfaction. It could be a small treat, a moment of rest, or a sense of success.

Observation

Consider your development regularly and the effects this practice has on your general well-being and productivity. Your commitment to the habit is strengthened, and this reflection improves your awareness of its advantages.

Routines centered on habits: Building blocks of productivity

Creating a habit-focused routine entails coordinating your everyday actions with your objectives and moral principles.

morning custom

Establish a morning routine to help you form good habits early in the day. This reduces the possibility of giving in to procrastination and establishes a positive tone for the remainder of the day.

Relaxation in the evening

Create a nightly schedule that helps you unwind. A disciplined nighttime regimen will improve your general health and set you up for success in the future.

Exercise: Describe Your Perfect Workday

Have you ever thought about what your perfect workday may entail? Which would you prefer—working in a busy office or from home? Would you work in a group or by yourself? Would you like to work on projects or attend meetings all day? You will be able to picture your ideal weekday and pinpoint the essential components that make it such with the aid of this exercise.

Step 1: Take a notebook or open a document on your computer, then give yourself ten minutes to complete it.

Step 2: Begin by imagining what your perfect workday may entail. Whatever comes to mind, no matter how minor, write it.

3. Pay attention to the specifics. When would you expect to awaken? What kind of morning routine would you follow? What sort of labor would you perform?

With whom would you collaborate? How would you set up your workspace? Try to be as detailed as you can.

Step 4: Review your brainstorming list and note the essential components of a productive workday. Is it the ability to work from any location? The capacity for teamwork and collaboration? The chance to work on difficult projects? Whatever it is, note it down.

Step 5: Examine how your work environment compares to your dream weekday. Do they differ, or are there any similarities? If there are discrepancies, can you adjust your work environment to match your ideal workday?

Step 6: Get going! Decide just one or two adjustments you can make to your workspace or workflow to align it with your ideal workday. Take initiative and begin streamlining your work process for success by designating a specific area for your workstation, modifying your work schedule, or figuring out how to cooperate more successfully.

There is no right or wrong way to create your ideal weekday; it is unique to you. Whether working on a project or trying to improve your work habits, this exercise can consolidate your work approach. You can obtain clarity on what you need to do to accomplish your goals and boost productivity by figuring out what your perfect workday looks like. Thus, enjoy the process, be creative, and have fun with it!

Master the Art of Giving Up

It can be difficult to let go of an emotional relationship with clutter, particularly when it comes to sentimental objects with deep personal meaning. It's crucial to understand, though, that keeping an excessive amount of clutter around can lead to worry and anxiety, which will impair your productivity and time management. An emotional attachment to sentimental objects is one of the main obstacles to managing disorder. I have personal experience with the difficulty of parting with treasured belongings. I used to cling to everything—from old letters from friends to toys from my childhood—believing that the memories and feelings connected to them were contained in these tangible items. But as my house and office got increasingly disorganized, I had more trouble concentrating and scheduling my time wisely. It's simple to become engrossed in the feelings and memories associated with these objects, which makes it difficult to let go.

It's crucial to stop and consider why these things are significant to you to overcome your emotional attachment to clutter. To preserve the memory, think about snapping a picture or jotting down a quick description of the item. Gratitude exercises might also assist you in concentrating on the memories connected to the object rather than the object itself. You can let go of the physical object while keeping the memory alive by valuing the pleasant memories and feelings it evokes.

Managing sentimental clutter also requires setting clear boundaries. Reduce the amount of sentimental items you own and periodically evaluate whether they are still meaningful. If an item is no longer useful, consider giving it to a good home or repurposing it into something beautiful.

Keeping an emotional distance from clutter is crucial to having a more productive and orderly environment. You can lessen tension and anxiety and enhance your productivity and time management by thinking back on the memories connected to sentimental objects, establishing clear boundaries, and gradually letting go of clutter. You may turn your disorganized workspace into a place of productivity and clarity if you adopt the appropriate techniques and mentality.

Cut off pointless meetings and concentrate on things that can be done.

Meetings are commonplace in the business world, frequently acting as vital spaces for ideation, judgment, and information sharing. But not every encounter is made equal. Unnecessary meetings can be major time, energy, and productivity wasters since they often lack specific goals or useful conclusions. By eliminating these pointless meetings and emphasizing actionable things, teams and individuals can increase productivity, create a more results-oriented work culture, and recover important time.

Analyzing each meeting's needs and goals critically is the first stage in this approach. Determine whether another channel—such as email, instant messaging, or a shared document—would be a more effective way to accomplish the same goal before setting up or accepting an invitation to a meeting. For example, written reports or bulletins that may be read at the recipient's convenience could take the place of meetings meant only to exchange information or offer status updates.

When a meeting is required, it ought to have a well-defined goal and schedule. This keeps the meeting on course and focused while assisting participants in their effective preparation. Each meeting should end with a clear set of action items, and every item on the agenda should directly contribute to the meeting's ultimate goal.

Moving from abstract ideas to specific plans and actions is what it means to concentrate on actionable items. A specified job or activity delegated to a specific individual with a deadline for completion is known as an actionable item. Meetings can become more productive and results-oriented by concentrating on these topics.

Think about implementing frameworks or instruments that promote action-oriented thinking to help with this. One possible way to conclude each meeting would be to summarize the action items discussed and allocate accountability for each one. To guarantee responsibility, these assignments should be documented and followed up on.

Furthermore, remember that not all tasks or decisions call for a meeting. It is possible to lessen the necessity for meetings and promote a climate of trust and accountability by giving people and groups the freedom to decide for themselves and to act. Similarly, encouraging effective communication can guarantee that all parties agree and lessen the requirement for meetings for clarification or alignment.

In conclusion, meetings can be important instruments for cooperation and decision-making, but they can also be time- and resource-consuming. A more effective, productive, and results-oriented climate can be established in the workplace by doing away with pointless meetings and concentrating on relevant issues. This method calls for a keen eye, sound judgment, and a dedication to responsibility and action. But the potential rewards—including time savings, higher productivity, and goal achievement—make the effort worthwhile.

When possible, automate repetitious chores.

Automation has become a potent tool for increasing productivity and efficiency in an era where technology quickly changes our operations. In the context of labor, automation is using technology to carry out monotonous tasks that would otherwise require a large investment of time and energy. By automating these tasks, you may free up important time for more intricate, imaginative, and strategic duties. These are the kinds of jobs that call for human judgment, creativity, and personal touch.

Data management is one of the most popular domains where automation is used. Automation solutions might be beneficial if your profession entails regular data entry or transmission. For example, you can use Zapier or IFTTT (If This Then That) to automate data transfers across applications or utilize Excel macros to automate data manipulation operations. This can entail updating a spreadsheet whenever a new entry is made in an online form or automatically moving email attachments to a cloud storage provider.

Another area that is prime for automation is email. For example, you can use rules and filters to automatically sort incoming emails, moving less important ones to a specified location and flagging crucial ones. Similarly, you can utilize prefabricated responses or templates to reduce the time you spend composing emails if you frequently find yourself responding to similar emails in different formats.

Moreover, automation can be utilized to improve collaboration and project management. Certain parts of project tracking and communication can be automated with the help of tools like Asana, Trello, or Jira. Examples of these automated processes include assigning tasks in response to specific trigger events or updating the status of linked tasks upon completion of one.

Keeping up your online presence is another area where automation can be helpful. Uploading fresh information or changes can be automated using scheduling software. Doing this lets you ensure that your digital platforms are interesting and current even while you're occupied with other things.

Recall that the purpose of automation is to free you up to concentrate on the jobs that call for your expertise, experience, and inventiveness rather than completely replacing the human element of work. Not all jobs lend themselves to automation; generally, leaving tasks requiring intricate decision-making, critical thinking, creativity, or a personal touch to humans is preferable.

Remember that the initial automation setup can need a significant amount of time and work. In the long run, though, they can save much more time once the mechanisms are in place.

To sum up, automation is an effective tactic for raising output and efficiency at work. You can save time, lower the possibility of mistakes, and free up your brain energy for more significant and rewarding duties by automating repetitive operations. The secret is determining which jobs can be automated, choosing the appropriate tools, and configuring your automation systems to best support your goals and workflow.

Being on time might help you grow in your career since businesses respect trustworthy workers.

Being punctual in a professional situation demonstrates to an employer your regard for their time and the significance of being on time for appointments. Being late for work or meetings can reflect adversely on your character, particularly in professions where on-time arrival is highly regarded.

For instance, arriving late for an interview could hurt your chances of getting recruited if the company prioritizes precision and responsibility.

They won't regard this as a desirable attribute in a potential employee.

You must arrive on time for both your personal and professional lives.

You must arrive on time for both your personal and professional lives. It demonstrates in a professional setting that you value other people's time and possess the self-control to keep your word. When individuals in social circumstances know what to expect from one another, the evening runs more smoothly.

We will discuss the value of punctuality in this chapter.

Being on time helps you avoid putting things off.

Being punctual involves being on time and keeping an eye on the time. Being on time will make you more conscious of how long tasks take and allow appropriate planning. Because there will be fewer needless delays, procrastination can be avoided by focusing on the task rather than on what must be done next. Being punctual also encourages people to take personal responsibility since, whether someone is late or early, they tend to rush through their tasks to be home in time for dinner or social engagements. When something happens frequently enough, it becomes a habit embedded in one's identity. Once someone has a history of taking responsibility and accountability for their actions (even if those actions are as simple as "being on time"), others will view them as dependable and trustworthy collaborators working toward shared objectives.

Pupils who arrive on time are more likely to receive higher grades.

Pupils who arrive on time are more likely to receive higher grades.

● If you arrive late, you might not be able to finish your work in time, and there's a possibility your teacher won't accept late assignments. Low marks may result from this.

You must develop your time management skills if you want to succeed.

Each of us has a finite amount of time. There are never enough hours in the day, whether you're a parent, worker, or student. You must develop good time management skills if you want to succeed in anything. What does this signify? Therefore, to ensure that everything runs properly and there is no last-minute rush, you should allow adequate time for your appointments if you want to be on time. Being on time also requires extra time for unforeseen events, which can occur at any time of day and include traffic jams and delays on public transportation. If these things happen, there won't be enough time for them, which could lead to missing crucial meetings or occasions, making it harder to accomplish objectives like graduating from high school or college or getting promoted at work.

Be considerate.

Contrary to popular belief, there are more advantages to being on time. Being on time demonstrates your organization, readiness, and regard for other people. It demonstrates to others that you are a trustworthy leader in the workplace.

Furthermore, individuals who arrive late get the impression that they are wasting their time, and nobody enjoys this feeling!

Acquire credibility.

Additionally, you're building a rapport of trust with your customers. Being on time demonstrates your regard for their time and willingness to go above and beyond for them. This is especially crucial in the business world, where clients may be extremely busy and have a lot on their plate at any given time.

If a client is confident in your punctuality, they are likely to assume that you will also manage other duties with professionalism. They won't have to worry about whether or not things will get done correctly because they know they can rely on you!

Appear well-organized.

● Make sure you bring everything you need.

● Prepare your supplies beforehand so you can go to work immediately, even if it means getting up a bit earlier than normal.

● Make sure you have all the necessary tools, supplies, and equipment for the task. This includes, in addition to your laptop and mouse, pens, paperclips, scissors, and tape (if applicable).

Lessen your tension.

● Avoid the frustration of missing appointments and meetings by arriving on time. Even if there are unanticipated delays, don't allow them to derail you; stick to your schedule. By doing this, you'll be able to resist the need to shift the blame elsewhere for your tardiness or initial forgetfulness of the appointment, which could lead to conflict and animosity between the parties. If you find yourself running late for an appointment or missing one altogether, don't try to justify yourself or brush it off. Instead, start by apologizing for any inconvenience caused and outlining the reason for any delays so that everyone knows what to expect the next time.

A common negative behavior that many people have is procrastination. Procrastination might be hard to resist, but it's crucial to do so because it can have negative long-term effects. Your reputation will take a hit if you skip an appointment or are late for work. If this keeps happening, you can also wind up losing your job. The greatest way to prevent procrastination is to schedule a period during the day to work on the tasks that need to be completed (like cleaning the house).

In order to make the most of your appearance, you must arrive on time.

Not only is punctuality courteous, but it's also essential to make the most of your presence. Consider this: Your boss might have to start the meeting without you if you are running late, and he will become distracted even before the meeting begins. Had someone else been allowed to speak first, he could have taken your place in the spotlight and damaged your reputation in front of the public.

Being late also reduces other people's time to prepare for whatever is happening. If your friend had been late for her graduation speech, she would have felt anxious as she stood in line with all the other graduates who had been considerate enough to arrive on time and wait patiently, as was expected of them (yes, these are all hypothetical situations). Anybody could become uneasy with that kind of tension!

Tips for Managing Your Time Well

1. Establish time-related priorities.

When someone struggles with time management, they spend more time on things that are not as vital as they should be. Being able to recognize and define your priorities is advantageous. Setting priorities lets you focus on your objectives and avoid distractions.

The age of social media is upon us. Information on the Internet is essentially exploding. Many websites and apps are out there; some might be useful to us, while others might just be there to kill time. There are no issues or concerns when you only want to kill time and spend it casually using some amusing apps, websites, or games. If you're at work and want to take a quick break before working on them, that's acceptable.

But even if you must work on something important, spending time on it could lead to problems because you would neglect a higher-priority task.

Here's an instance from my past, when I was younger:

Do you think a student can focus his time if he has an exam the next day and plays video games more than studying the day before?

That indicates that he can't set priorities. Yes, I was that student in high school. What resulted from my lack of capacity to set priorities in the past? Yes, I used to consistently have above-average grades, although, during my high school career, I failed one course.

It wasn't a case of my being an idiot and failing. Admitting that I was always a good student makes me feel wonderful. But regrettably, I did not study for long enough, especially during tests. I used to use my computer to play video games and become distracted. Luckily, I became aware of this mistake after high school.

I chose to major in IT engineering in college. I made it a point to balance having fun with studying during my engineering studies, and I ended up winning one of our class's semesters. It used to seem like a marvel that I could do that!

I don't hesitate to admit that there was a time when I didn't prioritize. Everyone experiences it. Human error occurs.

The most important lesson is that we must learn from our failures to improve as people and contribute to a brighter future.

How can you effectively manage your time?

The greatest methods to lessen this impact would be to

1. List the things you want to achieve.

2. Create a strategy to achieve.

You are more likely to follow through on your goals if you put them in writing.

It is not sufficient to just write down your goals; you also need to develop a plan that will outline exactly how you plan to achieve them. Regular progress reviews are essential once the plan is implemented. You may maintain your motivation to accomplish your goals by keeping track of your progress.

Writing down your goals is one of the most important "success secrets that can change your life."

2. Make it a practice to refuse requests from people.

Do you find it difficult to say no to people?

Do you prefer to say no to people but ultimately say yes to them?

There is no issue if you want to grant a favor that someone has requested. When you want to say no but are unable to, that is when the problem occurs. Saying no to others might seem easy, but breaking the habit is tough for those who struggle with it. This tendency hurts them, and they are occasionally afraid to say no to people. Not only does this lead to stress, but it also hinders their capacity to set priorities and efficiently allocate their time.

How can you start telling people no?

1. Determine the situations when you run into the issue.
Saying no to friends could be easier than to family or coworkers. If you can pinpoint the exact moments when the issue arises, solving it becomes simpler.
2. Start with tiny steps to get over your fear.
You can start taking little steps to solve the issue as soon as you've determined your situation.

Some of the following tactics are worth a try:

A. Provide a substitute

B. Justify your need to work on the assignment that is top priority.

C. When stating no, do it with grace and decency.

D. You might utilize the method you feel most at ease with, such as in-person interactions, email, WhatsApp, or SMS.

3. Preserve a Clear Workspace

A good time manager schedules a certain amount of time to organize their workspace. Thinking clearly when one's workspace or desk is cluttered is challenging.

Individuals with poor prioritization skills frequently put off doing tasks until later in life. Additionally, their workload and desks get crowded as time passes, making them feel more stressed.

How to Keep Your Workplace Clear of Clutter:

The first advice is to set a weekly time to clean your desk. Establishing a space for everything and arranging everything in its correct position. Remembering where to find certain things when you plan to preserve them in their original position is simpler.

Set aside space for stationery supplies, including pens, punching machines, staplers, etc. Store your files in a different place or folder. Those folders can be labeled or marked according to the kind of papers that are kept inside.

4. Allocate time in your calendar or weekly agenda for tasks involving poor time management.

Making time for the things you want to do is essential. The best approach is to create a weekly calendar or agenda. You can use a straightforward option, such as a notepad on your laptop or a diary.

The most important thing in this situation is using a simple solution that works for you.

5. Honor your word and don't back down from commitments

You have to fulfill your responsibilities. You will have a newfound respect for time when you recognize how important it is to keep your word.

At that point, squandering time or devoting effort to pointless activities gets more difficult.

You could try to figure out how long it will take you to complete your tasks. On top of that, you can add a 50% buffer for safety and emergencies. Next, give people promises. This will help you fulfill your responsibilities.

This is an illustration of what not to do:

My friend is employed in the field of information technology. He never stops talking to his coworkers during the day and isn't focused on completing the task. He continues to make false promises to his superiors and cannot finish his chores on time as the clock strikes four o'clock in the afternoon. This is because he suddenly realizes how much work he needs to perform.

Because of his poor time management, others suffer.

He always seems to be whining about how much work is at the workplace when, in reality, his poor time management is the true problem.

How to Become a Better Time Manager

When looking for work, you should demonstrate your superior time management abilities to potential employers. A hiring manager will find you more appealing if you highlight these skills on your CV.

The skills section of your resume is the most obvious location to emphasize your strengths in time management. This is the ideal place for someone to quickly review your resume and assess your level of expertise. On the other hand, your time management skills must be mentioned in the job descriptions under your Experience section. This enables you to be clear about how you applied your knowledge to meet deadlines and accomplish objectives. Thus, you're not just stating to a hiring manager that you possess these abilities; you're using them.

www.ingramcontent.com/pod-product-compliance
Lightning Source LLC
Chambersburg PA
CBHW050202130526
44591CB00034B/1813